Eclectic Electricity
unknown poet's parade

by Branch Isole

Copyright © 2013
Printed in the United States of America

Eclectic Electricity
unknown poet's parade
by Branch Isole

Library of Congress Control Number:
2010902252
ISBN 978-0982658512
eBook ISBN 978-0983574521

All rights reserved. No part of this publication may be reproduced or transmitted in any form or by any means without written permission of the publisher.

Manao Publishing
Hampton, VA 23666

Order copies of this book at
www.branchisole.com
www.manaopublishing.com

As a poet and storyteller I observe and comment on the motivations of our world both clothed and bare. Writing of adult issues and emotions often experienced but not always voiced, my style and presentation casts reflective identity against a backdrop of personal responsibility choice or avoidance. This is 'Voyeurism Poetry'.

Eclectic Electricity contains adult themes and language, some of which is erotic or sexual in nature and presentation. Eclectic Electricity is intended for mature audiences.

Voyeurism Poetry ~ looking out, seeing in ™

"Many write of things
known or experienced,
I comment on those seen and heard."

"Poetry only appears to be elitist,
its appeal is to every man."

Contents

5th & Mad
Absence
Aviator
Barfly Becky
Baseline
Black and Blue
Born of the Universe
Bull Shit
Clocking Out
Courting Disaster
Crowns
Cry Uncle
Double Jeopardy
Fantasia
Few and Fewer
Free Soul Rant
God's Many Ways
Grandchild
He Is . . . ?
Hell•th
Hottie
Inseparable
Irreversible
It Takes
John Eight Forty Seven
Kiddie Extortion

Knowledge
No Growth
No Bones About It
Ocular Peel
Offspring
One Heartbeat
Pilot
Preparation
Psycho Analysis
Queries
Relationship
Rut
Scribes
Secrets
See Saw
Six String
Symbolic
Taking Aim
Teen Show and Tell
The Most Important Word
The Point
The Way
The Word
Trash and Treasure
Twenty One
Why

Introduction

Writing and publishing has always been a difficult process and endeavor, and rightly so.

Today technological advancements have opened pathways of publishing to and for a worldwide audience. This has also brought out of the shadows untold numbers of writers.

Some writers become authors, a relative few become published and a handful may become recognized. In this way, publishing really hasn't changed at all.

Although technology has redefined the industry, good story telling and readership acceptance still determines each individual author's success.

If you are entertained or edified by the stories and poems herein, you are invited to discover more once this unknown poet's parade has passed by.

Branch Isole
the Voyeuristic Poet

"Publishing a volume of verse is like dropping
a rose petal down the Grand Canyon,
and waiting for the echo."

~Don Marquis

5th and Mad

Each generation is robbed of its innocence. . .
Evidenced by slide rule calculations
and emotionally stunted calibrations
Expressed as bloated Dickensian lives
Experienced within 'huddled masses'
Exploited by polity fascists

sacred
desperate
cunning,
running
scared

limping,
false bravado
unimpaired

fueled by insecurities
fostered by entitlement
fed by 5th and Madison

Absence

Days grow shorter
the end times approach
our struggles increase
Your children look
to you for relief,
Still you do not answer

We've known four hundred years of silence
twice experienced without you
your back turned in disgust
Our convenient lifestyles
daily tests for us

Crying out for release
for guidance,
answers
You respond as you please;
as rock
solid stone
only your back exposed
from upon your throne

Is it the false prophets
we choose to follow
or the carnality
in which we wallow
Keeping hidden from our view
muffling our ears
silencing you

You gaze into our hearts
filled with science and art
a burgeoning, blistering world
the home of lust and greed
its festering pustules bleed
spreading covetous cankers
as ripened roots of disease

We shout out your name
then spit upon it, taking it in vain
when you fail to acknowledge us,
immediately

Aviator

Flight,
from Icarus to Wrights
Boeing and beyond
progressive steps for man
in ventured forth movements
conquering the ethereal

Released, unbound
free once more
to leave the ground

to float
to stream
at the speed of soul
traversing distances extreme
both great and small

Barfly Becky

She flutters,
bar stool to stool
Imbibing, becoming
a drunkard's fool

Believing herself a butterfly
of establishment's seductive genre
Insecurities pitted deep within
keep her cold as tundra

She's every girl's girlfriend
but a real man hater
the truth be told
Yet her obsessive compulsion
for daddy's love later
requires she never
home alone goes

Sacrificially to each
she offers herself up
Talking constantly
running her mouth
Preparing her head
to slowly go south

The only murmuring
these men want to hear
from her incessant pleas to please,
is soft humming
of pursed lips
while down on her knees

She calls herself Lil
the computer techie
but everyone knows her
as Barfly Becky

Baseline

There are no more degrees of hypocrisy,
than there are of sin

Black and Blue

From out of the blue
From the black of past
You return

As if deposited,
the result of a shooting star's streak?
or the impact of a murderous comet?
Both tempt and repel this onlooker
whose life took many twists and turns
away from you

ever so innocently
re-establishing the link,
a piquant connection to spark interest
alluding to charms long ago enjoyed
whose stature must still fully arrest

Yes, you were delicious to behold
Your sacrifice would have mortared
a loose bond,
but caught off guard
and unprepared
cemented failure

And Now?
What of Now?
Baited, is that your plan?

You cast a long line of tackle offerings;
glistening
shimmering
in the light of night
or day

either, you say
and you are believed

in the open or clandestinely
you are ready,
willing,
to risk again
being bruised

Black and Blue

Born of the Universe

Here we are...

"You ain't nobody,
 'cept to you"

Or is that,
It's Up To You...?!

Bull Shit

Wall Street is the world's religion
and as with all religions
is built on a perception
and belief that,
at its core is truth.

Clocking Out

Tick Tock

What cruelty, Fate
to discover at long last
purposeful desire
and simultaneously to find
this clock's precisely honed mechanics
ticking,
winding steadily down

No longer balanced normality
ne'er a glint
nor redaction thereof,
so tautly askew
its main spring wound

Requesting new found acceptance
enough time to make things right
Frightened to close these weary eyes
at the mercy of peril and strife
Fearing the darkness enveloping
prior to new morning's light

Praying for revelation
of new understanding's new way
Life now a twelve-step program
consigned day to day

Anticipation naught
of the journey ahead
Destination accepted
fully shown
Single regret
a recurring thought
No time left
on this biological clock

Tick
Tock

Courting Disaster

When he's trying so hard
go ahead,
give in,
a little
Place a peck on his cheek
Not so as to distract
but as impetus to spur him onward
Further down the path of adoration
with attempts to please
Along the lane of courtship
he appreciates a good tease
It keeps his attentiveness in tune
and at the same time on edge

Enjoy the unmitigated gifts
lavished in heat's pursuit,
for once comfortable familiarity
drapes its unsettled self
only memories will flourish
with the glitter of gemstones
and the flowering beauty of spring

Allow him to fall on the sword of fate
in an expression of undying gratitude
exchanged for one or two soft swoons
or coy glances, released in his direction

His declarations of devotion
spoken in haste
ignited by the fires of passion
smoldering in his loins,
driving him temporarily mad
will not long be remembered
or revisited
after the eruption of his conquest
has been spent

Herein, the die is cast
the game lost
if your guard of aloofness be lowered
drawn down to the footstool of his actualization

Shackled by the grasp of his insecurities
Condemnation to a lifetime of servitude
surely follows

Crowns

how is it Lord
You unseen, unheard,
yet the fulfillment within my heart
is as no other
when You are in my thoughts

the peace and understanding of our roles…
yours and mine
is at no time
more precise, more clear
than when You bless me
with communion
of our two spirits

it is when You invite me
to rediscover your presence
within my life and world
that your crown of glory
takes its rightful place
in my heart
above all carnal and material desires

it is these meditative moments of reflection
one by one
like droplets of water upon limestone
which wear away and erode
the rough surface of my porous existence
revealing the smooth void created,
which once more may be filled
only with and by You,
its creator

Cry Uncle

God I'm so over you
strung along from pillar to post
elevated pinnacle highs
with summit swirls of illusion
perpetrated to bring me down
cowering in submission
to prove what point,
your superiority?

You, all powerful in this relationship
yet the strength of your authority
depends upon my submissive acquiescence,
otherwise, what have you actually gained?

Your humble presentation
masks a wrath of purpose
Except that it is your perpetuation, not mine
Should I fade into oblivion, who is disappointed
You or me?
You I fear.

For you shall go on
recognizing and understanding loss
while I will have become
but a distant memory
passed to nothingness, to all except you

then will you cry for me?
Unconditionally?

Double Jeopardy

Questions, Questions, Questions
Ask and you'll be told
Seek and you will find
filling yours as they empty theirs'
powers of the mind

File away important notions
disregard the fluff
whenever their wagging tongues start with "I"
you realize you've heard enough

Every Pulitzer knows
five W's say it all
total, beginning to end
yet when talking story
trust neither foe nor friend

Today's fax, not the facts
dot matrix speed of light
prints across the land
fancy, fantasy holds each reader's rapt
short attention span

celebrity induced coma
intra-fed naked idiocy
grading away, dumbing down
to a blasé fifth

one more wager
for spotlight craving hounds
of '15 minutes' they never tire

Speaker
Listener
Talker
Hearer
Liar, Liar

Fantasia

Subject broached,
times over the years
Agreement,
if there was a 'No'
from any one of three
born of fear or hesitancy
progression further
could
should
would
not be

Baring that
allow curiosity
to enthrall the cat

Nerves subsiding
Looks all around
small talk, touches
heat rising
fantasies abound

Tongues, Lips
Shafts, Tips
Thumbs, Fingers
pleasures linger
Him in her
Her in them
Twisting, Twirling
making heads spin

Filling each other up
with his, with her
licentious smiles
salacious purrs
Restrictions abandoned
once and for all
total sharing
caring
having a ball

One and one and one
make three
sated complete, thoroughly
Each one's
forbidden fruit
picked from the tree

Few and Fewer

When you're gone
Few will know
Fewer still will care…

On your day
one or two may remember and smile,
what more could you hope for?

Free Soul Rant

Life,
what an interesting show to watch
seeing how people
will shear off their noses
to spite their face
I wonder what it is
leading to that place.

Is it our need to be right
all of the time,
or are we afraid
we might look inept
by asking a foolish question?
As if we are so important
that others would pay us attention
Hanging in silence
on our every word,
as each syllable rolls slowly
from our tongues and lips
like sap of the maple
If that were the case
we would be secure within ourselves,
and we know we are not.

We are just as insecure
as those who have multiple
tattoos and piercings,
which invite and instigate
people to look
to stare,
to wonder;

what in the world
compelled them to do that
to their bodies?
And subsequently
subconsciously
to their minds,
other than the fact
their insecurity
by their markings, screams it!

But then, we already knew that,
having been exposed to their incessant
preening and parading
for attention.

We, who are
'too embarrassed to ask a foolish question'
are just as insecure.
We simply don't own that 'in your face' attitude
or (im)maturity
to risk potential
self-inflicted physical pain
or the social stigma
of laughter.

We are not prepared
to leave home each day
on the offensive.
We have spent too many years
honing our battery of excuses,
which are ready
at a moment's beck and call

to be drawn out
as fast as a gunslinger's pistol
decorated with telltale notched victories
upon the grip.

We are much more comfortable
waiting and lurking,
in order to get and keep
the upper hand of control
in each and every situation.

To us, winning the battle
and losing the war
means that from the grave
we may still pompously claim
in a whispered shout,
"At least I won the battle."

We must presume
(for we never assume,
as we both know
what happens there)
We presume
they have never heard,
None
no, not one
of the hundreds
of motivational speakers
or "life coaches"
(are you kidding me?)
from virtually every field
of endeavor

who at least once
in every performance
remind the audience,
"there is no such thing
as a foolish question."
(still no response)

Have we been cloistered
in some little room
with remote in hand,
the TV tuned
to a twenty-four/seven cable channel
"Reality TV - (Really)"!?

or perhaps,

We are afraid to
discover something new
which we might truly enjoy.
God forbid!
which might shake up
our comfortably numb and safe existence,
whereby we might actually grow
from the experience.

No, better we wake each morning
with our prepared and planned responses
which fit nice and neat
into our pre-conceived notion of normalcy,
for after all, that is normal for us.
No matter how mundane
our life may be.

That's what plausible deniability
and closets full of skeletons
are about.

Don't fret
we can go on dreaming
hoping we never actually have to risk
stepping outside the box,
coloring outside the lines,
or living free enough
to make a decision
allowing us to be wrong
and still awaken
tomorrow morning.

We dare not venture there,
for to do so would show
that our life will not end
and our mother or father
will not be disappointed,
as we actually risked
making a decision
which prompts us
to try something new
and growth filled.
However, that then
begs the question-
What will we do
with the whips and chains
in our closets,
when we stop
beating ourselves up

as we become more aware
of our inner soul
in order to actually live
and change the things
which pain and disgust us
about ourselves?
After all, if we knew and believed
each decision is ours
and it's okay to decide,
even if the outcome
is different
than we thought it,
should be
could be
would be
or that we might make a mistake
and be wrong . . .

What would the world
of pharma psycho-babble do,
with one less
free soul?

God's Many Ways

Debates rage
on and on
years, decades
centuries pass
Each side struggles
its providential need to be right
Ecclesiastic preparations
for their next crusading fight

East versus West
Buddha versus Christ
Muslim and Jew
Atheist, Agnostic
Wiccan too
Each has a personal stake
Each lives, consumed by
a parochial view

Reincarnation for example,
there's a topic intermittently hot
Eastern philosophy says
why yes, of course,
Christianity, no way
Never, not!

Biblical scripture clearly states
"but once to live is a man's fate"
this its readers do behold
yet true if this recorded line may be
does 'one lifetime' apply
to both body *and* soul?

If who we are
in reality is,
cosmic energy
temporarily occupying
physical time and space
Is it not possible
a spirit filled soul
might acquire levels
and opportunities to express
experiencing truth and love
while on the way
to a place above
where streets are said
to be paved with gold?

Take for instance
one Christian scholarly belief
that the 'Angel of the Lord'
of Old Testament fame
is actually the Holy Spirit forerunner
of a different New Testament name

If that Old Testament Angel,
the singular one
sent by the Lord God
appeared at different times
in human form
before many and separate
Old Testament men,
returning each time as Holy Spirit
Was not that Spirit incarnate,
again and again?

Jumping ahead
a few thousand years
to the time of Empirical Rome's
persecution fears
A tribal people
inhabiting Canaan
one of their own genealogical peers
hung on a cross
representing humanity's temporary loss

Death on a cross
one man who did leave us
One believed in and followed
his name was Jesus

Gone…
only to return, once again,
in body and soul he was seen
for weeks on end
by followers both women and men

And then to leave them
He heaven bound
yet again

Jesus, who lived and died
As seen by the many who testified
They had witnessed with their own eyes

As was recorded more than once
through Old Testament times
and into the New,
His Spirit incarnate
time and again
each time becoming
made into man

And so too today
this truth believed
by Christian multitudes
of each and every nation

Explain please now
if you would,
the definition of, reincarnation

Grandchild

Apple of my eye
Desire of my heart
Experiencing moments as you grow
memories that we share
Secrets known by only we two
these joys are but a few
you bring into my life

Seeing my child, your parent
and a little of my own
similar characteristic traits
familial antics, movements, tones

Natural dispositions of a genetic three
part and parcel passed
through our family tree

You test the bounds of love
Stretch patience from inch to mile
Yet disavowment melts to nothing
Overpowered by your smile

Captivated by your innocence
Confounded by such honesty
One moment angelic
the next rough and raw
No matter what you say or do
all retrospective redeemed
by a whisper of "I love you"
Grandpa

~for Maya

He Is . . .?

either God exists or he doesn't.

if he does
then *evolution* is his growth and change process

(for him to create *all* in six days
would prove
he is who he claims to be,
an undeniable Omnipotent entity)

if he doesn't
what's the point?

Hell•th

Unable to recall the vibrant hubris of youth
variegated maladies now take turns
ravaging her emotional verve
with pent up foreboding
of potential destruction
by her psyche's
impending migraine strain

Remembering days when 'health'
was a mere word
denoting scenarios afflicting others
in distant impoverished lands
or individuals teetering
on the far edge of chronology

Kaleidoscope reminders of
muscle
joint
organ
discomfort
now take center stage
in rejoinders of occupation,
plying alternate moments of angst
and prayerful meditation

The hourglass tipped, then conversely righted
allow the sands of time to tumble steadfast,
pushing against themselves
through a constricted sphincter of pain
Nevermore to be relegated solely
by cerebral folds of the brain

Until all systems are at peace with one another
while perched upon the precipice
of a single final heartbeat

before the stillness of exhaustive rest
sighs relief,
and breathes life into decay

Hottie

Sizzlin' baby
that's what you are
When my tips rake your skin
sparks fly
heat rises
blood begins to boil

Charged are you,
exuding sultry sensuality
and comely sexiness

Your aura of surrounding femininity
sprayed as if cosmic rays of energy
beguiles every transfixed eye
drawn in your direction

To have those supple lips slightly parted
a flicking tongue
removing the drop of sweetness
produced by the welling anticipation
of your naked touch,
balancing it for the world to see
before tasting and swallowing
this man made nectar

Straddled atop
ears muffed by silky smooth thighs
staring longingly at your bare mound descending
smothering lips with lips
my tongue searches the sides
which lead upward
to your hooded hidden button
the 'key' to your first stage of pleasure

You electrify my being
as we are joined
our puzzle completed
by penetration and reception
Backs arch as souls scream aloud
and we become one
bucking in unison
until flung afar into solitudes of ecstasy
by orgasmic explosions and release

Bodies flameless fire
radiating desire
produces pools of liquid love

Stroking, stoking
the repository of rekindled embers
of our next ablaze position

Inseparable

Each holiday and season
brought requests and gifts
Toys, candies, clothes and games
electronics, equipment
newer models, more of the same

Coveted material things
under trees, in bags
most wrapped, others not
expectant exchange, symbols love fraught

Where are those prized possessions today?
What closet, attic, basement or trunk
keeps them safe, protects their aging,
promoting their wasting away

the "have to haves" of long ago
the "I can't live without" for one more day
how much time, money, energy was invested
to be 'first on the block'
to be the one 'never bested'

And now?
What can I possibly give, influence or desire
that of itself you will never tire?
Guaranteeing our continuance
as spiritual parent and offspring
what singular gift to you can I bring?
One of encouragement, responsibility
to exhibit love's encapsulating civility

None past nor present
nay, not one
can stand in comparison
to that I wish to share
for you to own,
to spend eternity with you
before the eyes on God's throne

Irreversible

Your action was deemed reprehensible
Now it, you cannot retract
How long will you ruminate
beat yourself up?
mentally flogging, stripping the seared
stripes of skin from your back

Who was it that called you 'stupid'
Who decorated your mind's stage
with a punishing harshness of curse
lorded over you
chastising, convincing,
proclaiming "there are none worse"

You vocalized words
pronounced inappropriate
Now there's no un-ringing the bell
Who informed you speaking
truth from the heart
is deemed to be unacceptable

Perhaps it is,
in self-righteous circles
of stigmata social structure,
but someone must step up
and prick their balloon
with adequate pressure to puncture

You stretched the bounds
now you're in deep
a protracted gnawing abyss
Who was it
rather than help you out
stepped on your fingers
at the rim's upper lip

and so it goes for those,
who give in rather than risk

It Takes

The writer's job
is to write everyday
regardless of if or not
there is something to say

It takes exercise,
as important as that
of a body building Mr. Universe

It takes practice,
ad nauseam
until the surgeon wants to curse

It takes the tenacity,
of a Nubian lover
who has eyes and heart
for no other

It takes the patience of Job,
bringing a project to completion
It takes the particularity
of a master chef
who continues to strive
for needed revision

It takes the security
of a seasoned
Lady of the Night
assisting 'the john'
experience his first time

It takes the commitment
of an athletic coach's
unwavering dedication
to the team's important
game preparation

Most of all
It takes faith
and true belief
that out there, somewhere
is a reader or two
moved to stir up a buzz

For in their lives
they face constant rejection
The same
as the writer does

John Eight Forty Seven

You have but requested
we recognize your name
yet modern day apostles
coerce through guilt's shame

Unable to accept balance
on the path of peace
their goal, separation
keeping you and we at extremes

Their declarations of you;
Wrath
Compassion
unattainable,
Forgiveness

Yet it is we who give them power
to decide our fate
it is we who allow their extortion
of our emotional state

Never your way
truth be told
Only one intermediary between you and us
One teacher, advocate, lord
He who went to the cross

This glut of self-righteous
false prophets unnecessary
in order to belong to you,
for you have explained simple and true
our instructions from heaven
understand the relationship proclaimed
in John 8:47

Kiddie Extortion

Our neighborhood kids
have fund raising skills
running the gamut
from pint sized know nothings
to con artist shills

Whether cookies, candy
magazines or fruit
each little Dale Carnegie
and Napoleon Hill
leaves me mute

What can I say?
when it's their parents
my friends,
who deliberately
steer them my way

I can say yes
or I could say no
the choice is entirely mine
My take on it is, as if it were
an obligatory community fine

It's like paying for protection
with a box of cookies thrown in
"By the way, do you have any more
of those delicious chocolate mint thins?"

One more expenditure
Another little fee
paid to live on my block
Part and parcel
of neighborhood living
within this community flock

They're enterprising
at least they try
and once each year
I manage a pittance payback

For each Halloween
I elicit their screams
as the dismembered man
tied to the rack

Knowledge

The most valuable attribute in the world
is knowledge,
from it, all else springs into being

Ideas are the seedlings
of knowledge
Intellectual properties
the living waters
of nurture and growth
which, through expression
the world as we know it
comes into existence
In an ongoing revolution
of progressive application
we use, abuse
and build upon

It is knowledge which creates
problems
solutions
challenges

Knowledge;
The man without it, struggles
The man with it, toils
The man who mixes it
with spiritual understanding
and an acknowledgment of God
may be blessed to experience wisdom

No Bones About It

In today's world
you know you've "arrived"
when your 'skeletons' are more important
than your contribution.

In today's world
You know you're over exposed
when your 'skeletons' are
the most important association
with your name.

Not until your 'skeletons' live again
do you become
one of "them"

No Growth Zone

Self-centered behavior
exhibits itself as ignorance
For it lacks comparison
beyond self

Ignorant behavior
most often expresses itself
as rudeness
For it lacks comparison
beyond its environment

Crude behavior is seen
when self-centered,
ignorant,
rude people
lack maturity
and the will or desire to grow,
beyond themselves
their behavior
or their current surroundings

Ocular Peel

your disciples love to proselytize;
your Omnipotent control
according to a plan,
that all are accepted
by Omnipresent forgiving eyes

if stone hearted pharaohs be necessity;
to empower each Moses' stuttering words
because your children
turn away, refuse
through ebbing flows of their own,
why not enlighten the Devil's given,
their earned dues

even You
can't have it
both ways

covenant Apostle claimants;
your Word true told
suffering your promise
against a world's indifference
caring not one way or the other
the struggles cuckold
within your fold

sending One to save the sinners;
condemning free will
you chose to give,
your stymied efforts
against a preponderance of proof
does Jobian faith, yet still live?

prescriptive control;
disruptive choice or election
to remain under a thumb,
damning disdain
you abjectly objected
relinquishing your own son

at odds;
the guilt of conscience
you supplied
against the tests,
for your forgiving eyes

Offspring

Truth
is the proving ground
of Love

in our search for worthiness

to stave off indifference
and disappointment

of our recognition

for approval

One Heartbeat

Which is it calling to us
and stirring the essence
that lives within?
Is it the rhythmic tempo or the driving beat?
the Beat. . . must be the Beat
It's always the Beat
the Beat
the Beat

The Beating of war drums
or the peace drum present
The Beat of the drum, The Beat of the drum
In good times and bad
Same instrument, different meanings.
Life . . . and . . . Death
Same cycle, different names.

Pilot

Many days and nights have we traveled together
always have I relied upon you
for me, ne'er a care
with you at the controls

Warm and comforted have I been
no matter the weather
nor influences outside
while transported here and there
relaxed was I

all needs met
by your sanguinary blessed vessel,
announcing my presence
awaiting arrival
an appearance to be revealed

Sense of woman
Strength of man
these you gave
with the kiss of your breath,
by the touch of your hand

no rejection
my election
Understanding your love
accompanies me
as I follow the amniotic flood
of emotionally charge fluid
flowing before me

Still the Pilot
of my soul's heart
until the stain of mankind
blots and absorbs me
as part of the dark

Preparation

Between
the essence of who we become
and the extraction of whom we were
lies opportunity

Influenced by angels and demons
of our own making
manifested in response and (re)actions
to the people and events in our lives
Triggering layers of self
to be alternately exulted or obscured
trumpeted by heralds, hidden in the shadows

Scurried and scattered
along the circuitous route of choices
guiding or misleading us down the path
Understanding burns as a candle
in the light of the sun

and yet,

spark ignited
fueled by experience
prepares for launch against the strain and draw
of the cosmos

enveloped by spirit's loving arms
or cast aside
beyond eternity's arm's length reach

Breathed by heart's, mind's speech
Our ticket to freedom
announced and collected
by our one word answer

Yes
or
No

Psycho Analysis

The artist glimpses growth
when works from the past
revisit,
and encounter a blasé reception
where once they were deemed
exquisite

The artist's compulsion;
Exposure
Testing publicly
perceptions of truth

'Tis genre and style,
culprit and cohort
who seek an audience

Queries

When the delusions
of communal participation
no longer sustain a cursory understanding
of entering by birth
and exiting by death
alone,
The struggles perpetrated in between
become self-evident
through their own clarity
of exhaustion and effort

Now may the individual construct
become a formulation
asked and answered;
Why am I here?
Do I now know?

Relationship

Where God is
There is forgiveness
Where forgiveness is
There is understanding
Where understanding is
There is compassion
Where compassion is
There is a shared sense of vulnerability
Where this shared sense exists
There is knowledge of oneness
Where oneness dwells
There is a communion of love
Within a commune of love
Truth may thrive
Where truth is
The essence of spirits
Identify with each other

This is why I love you

for CC

Rut

You live life vicariously
expressing self
through your own vivid experiences
Peppered like 'shot' at every opportunity
Scattering anticipation of identification
by others
that you might become
more acceptable to them
and therefore, to yourself

Self-righteous indignation and scathing glee
bathed in visage of others' potential failure
props you up as one duped
by self-delusion

You miss the mark
of conversation's relativity
not because you don't know,
but because you won't listen,
prior to inserting yourself full fledged
into the bespoken mix
whereby you conceal a trap
set for any and all,
yet you are the one snared

forcing a cower from the glare
of the spotlight you desirously crave

Refusing to listen, learn and grow
overshadowing embarrassment is cast headlong
across the deepened hole
from which you continue to dig
down,
instead of out

Scribes

Fiction's task, to entertain
through foretold lore, story, plot
While "Non" educates, instructs,
its structure exceedingly taut

the Poet's charge;
pry loose the reader's heart,
exposing it to light of day
or night's opaqueness dark

allowing the reader to then reclaim it
hence known
"I am not alone"

Secrets

A comfort will be missed
Secrets two have shared
Minute aspects of daily life
Souls which have been bared
Vulnerabilities long ago breached
Fodder now for emotions that seethe

An undercurrent recently present
yet blinders disallowed peripheral introspection
Leaving produces heartbreak
but will abandonment
initiate greater pain
than an eventual knowledge
of a vowed trust decimated
piece by piece
incident by incident
behind one's back

Rewards and punishment
hover clandestinely within the shadows
each waiting to be revealed
A power struggle balanced precariously
atop the apex of promises made
while impatience gnaws
upon the fortitude of belief

At what point
are the pangs of voluntary servitude broken
only to be supplanted
by the loneliness of independence
At what level
the depth of love?

See Saw

how often is it
with our hopes, our dreams
requesting aide and comfort
guidance and strength
we turn to the Lord

with a pinch of favoritism, reward
bringing to fruition
our self-centered need to serve
(who?)

that God would know and understand
our desires,
are in His best interest

Surrendering…
but not

Feeling abandoned
we turn from the Lord
Acquiescing
we will accomplish all
on our own!
recognizing our inabilities
we flirt with the world
and its ways

to obtain that which we want
melded within private visions
of outcomes,
temptations

With veiled attempts
to be convinced
of the greater good
it represents…
to God
to Man
yet always to ourselves

Convincing us of our need
Believing our paramount pinnacles
grounded in linkage
to the prevaricated identity
we have broadcast…

from the mirror
to the world

Six String

Learned to play
while in rehab
given an old six string
by the girl from the lab
Mastered several
chords and riffs,
made them all
tight as a fist

Listened to addicts
tell tales of woe
about scoring hits
of horse and blow
Put them together
one snippet at a time
Worked to make
each of them rhyme

Eight months later,
off crack
and the bong
Came out cleansed, armed
with a catalogue of songs

Now it's travel,
traveling tours
playing one night gigs
some small, others big

To him it makes no matter
how many people show
declaring sincerely
he'd still go,
and play a concert
for one lonely soul like me
If it keeps him away from
those rehab clinic slugs
and off all those
desirable drugs

Symbolic

It was necessary for Jesus of Nazareth
to live and die in an era
when the executioner's tool was the cross

For no other symbol of demeaning elevation
could have evolved to have such impact

Taking Aim

You aim to please
For you, a state of being
bending your position
as you see it, 'over backwards'

your need to please
recognition
approval
how far back does it go?
from whence did it grow?
what part of that tree
maternal, paternal
has kept you
bound?
from being free?

And now you purpose it
upon us
with every query we have
Paws in the air, panting
emotional explosion held at bay
awaiting each response
to make your day. . .
or destroy it

We love you, we understand
it's just who you are
but our love endeared
is not dependent upon acceptance
as it was for years
with those genetically disposed
by whom you were reared

Teen Show and Tell

She's struttin' sway back
and standing tall
Protruding pretentious points
leading her way
Postured intentions
producing male enticements
with erectile risings

Small firm breasts
Supple young teats
Pert
Perky
Arresting

Showing expanses of
bronzed terra cotta
soft porcelain skin
Desperate for man's
wanton desires
to handle
stroke
and fondle them

Directed at man's muted
lust filled genital mustering
Her power, the pain
of Blue Ball busting

Staring straight ahead
searching for admirers without moving her head
her seeking eyes in unison click
while moving theirs and the pulsating tips
of their hardening pricks

Cautiously hoping
Tentative prayer
One might like to lick
and insert his bulging bulbous heat
deep,
inside her wet, sticky
candied sweets

Movements by long practiced design
Her seductive slither
A look of come-hither
created solely
for a cum-all-over-me appeal
Teasing each mentally
to cop a feel

Virginity intact
She struts away
sway back

The Most Important Words

Ten. Love God first and most,
treat your neighbor as yourself

Nine. If you knew me,
you would know my Father

Eight. You can not serve both God and money

Seven. I am the resurrection and the life

Six. The truth will set you free

Five. Go and sin no more

Four.   This is my son

Three. Love each other

Two. Jesus Christ

One God

The Point

I don't find your promises attractive
Anymore, than your denials for not finding the
Time, it would take to show I am still
Important, enough to make the struggle
worthwhile

It's redundant
Starting over
After accepting the sacrifice and then
Excusing, it as a substitute for fulfillment
as if it had
Meaning, beyond you and me

You never stray but your
Ever present, guilt trip
Hovers, over my shoulder
Possessing, a disparaging smirk

You indicate
Desire, to share my success yet you raise the
Bar, all efforts which take me closer to
Rewards, you change by altering the
Parameters, of acceptance
As I draw nearer to each goal

Exactly what is
the Point, you're trying to make?
that if you help insure my failure your
Unconditional love, becomes more evident?

To whom?
You or me?

Which of your justifications lead you to believe
Continuation, would entice me to be with you
in the future?

The Way

Service.
Now there's a word
many use, wear
and proudly proclaim,
their motivation
a discordant sense of duty
a cost of playing the game

Ask or not
they'll tell you why
the many ways it does apply
to them, this, their lauded recognition gem
followed by excruciating details
suffered and endured
along their path to martyrdom

Truth be told
Reciprocity
is never far from mind
It's the channel, the gauge
the measuring stick
protracting the distance
the twists, the bends
they're willing to sojourn

While the only part
coming from their heart
is how to receive
their self-perceived
acceptable rate of return

The Word

Open my mind Lord
that i might know Your Word

Cleave the lobes and folds
as Abram did with his covenant sacrifice
that your spirit may pass between
these symbols of surrender

Live within my tissue and blood
as You did with Abraham
Wash clean with crimson Lord
the stain of gray
matters

Open my heart Lord
that i might learn Your Way

That Your Spirit would have
a new place to dwell
joining together my existence
of the physical and spiritual
between this world and Yours

Open my eyes Lord
that i might see Your Truth

Make clearer
the distinction between self and righteous
as i look in the mirror
may Your Truth stare back
through these windows to the soul
against the glare of the world

Open my arms Lord
that i might embrace Your being

Through the senses
Your presence
surrounds me
with all Your creations
Called to serve You Lord
I AM
Guide

and guided by
Thoughts of You

signs and markers
dotting the path,
stretch before
like a ribbon of fear
into the black
(un)known
as future

Trash and Treasure

A lone palm frond
hangs limp
from the heat
of a noon day sun
Yielding slowly
each day marks a journey
from green to burnished gold

Twisted by the wind
valiantly trying
Doing its best
to keep from dying

More water?
Shade from another
closely planted neighbor?
A cool evening breeze?
What would it take
to be revitalized,
to be redeemed?

Turned to mulch
to dust, to ash,
to be composted
as green waste trash

To be re-mixed,
in an eco-waste bin
Part of new life
for other seed
bud or bulb

Remixed
and born again

Twenty One

Many people
particularly the young
think adulthood miraculously begins,
at twenty-one
When they self-indulgently celebrate
and sing a birthday song,
more often however
they are totally wrong

Adulthood isn't dependent
upon any particular chronological age
or how long it takes
to outgrow the onset
of one's juvenile behavioral phase

Neither is it designed
as a long awaited gift of life
Nor a tag team effort
when one takes a spouse,
be it husband or wife

Adulthood doesn't bloom
when one starts optioning
self-centered choices
Or decides to finally participate
in all the adult courses

Adulthood doesn't start
when you stop being selfish
Or are willing to be responsible
For your own decisions

Adulthood dawns
the day you realize
there's no way to undo
the damage you've brought
by the selfish
behaviors, choices
and decisions previously wrought

Why

I shot myself this morning
How fucked up was that
Pulled the trigger
in the bathtub
so as not to make a mess

Desired not pain
nor anguish be caused
needed to unlade the load
Carrying eighty hours per week
couldn't take the stress

Know you'll do, get along fine
no longer space for us
out of the way
needed peace,
from this maze
one last release

Overcame the fear of the moment
Realized it all must end
Too far distanced to explain
In too deep to extricate
No longer prisoner to the pressure
No longer caring to make amends

What difference is it
how we're taken
from the expectations of others, of self
no longer bound and tied
penultimate expression of self-criticism,
decision; suicide

Branch Isole is the author of nineteen books. Born in Osaka Japan, Branch Isole traveled extensively growing up calling many places home. Finishing high school in Rolling Hills, California he went on to graduate from Texas State University San Marcos, attended graduate school at the University of Houston and received an M.A. Theology degree from Trinity Bible College and Seminary, Newburgh Indiana.

Branch Isole's catalogue of work includes books, eBooks, greeting cards, inspirational gift mats, available at:

www.branchisole.com
www.manaopublishing.com

Other books by Branch Isole
Poetic Prose Series

Epigram ©
long story short
ISBN 978-0982658574
eBook ISBN 978-0983574576

Heartstrings of Illusion ©
Distractions and Deceit in Poetic Prose
ISBN 978-0982658543
eBook ISBN 978-0983574545

Dreams and Schemes ©
Tales and Tattles in Poetic Prose
ISBN 978-0982658550
eBook ISBN 978-0983574552

In The Margins ©
where truth lies
ISBN 978-0982658536
eBook ISBN 978-0983574538

Turn Of A Phrase ©
Pivotal Positions in Poetic Prose
ISBN 978-0982658505
eBook ISBN 978-0983574514

Saccharin and Plastic Band Aids ©
Comments in Poetic Prose
ISBN 978-0974769288
eBook ISBN 978-0983574453

Messages In A Bottle ©
Inspirations in Poetic Prose
ISBN 978-0974769295
eBook ISBN 978-0983574446

Reflections On Chrome ©
Parking Lot Confessions in Poetic Prose
ISBN 978-0974769257
eBook ISBN 978-0983574422

Postcards from the Line of Demarcation ©
Points of Separation in Poetic Prose
ISBN 978-0974769264
eBook ISBN 978-0983574439

Seeds of Mana'o ©
Thoughts, Ideas and Opinions in Poetic Prose
ISBN 978-0974769219
eBook ISBN 978-0983574415

Barking Geckos ©
Stories and Observations in Poetic Prose
ISBN 978-0974769226
eBook ISBN 978-0983574408

Orgy of Words ©
Salacious Short Stories in Poetic Prose
ISBN 978-0982658529
eBook ISBN 978-0983574569

<u>Spiritual Christianity Series</u>

Even Christians Stumble and Fall ©
Musings of a Struggling Believer
ISBN 978-0974769240
eBook ISBN 978-0983574491

Crucibles ©
Refinement of the Neophyte Christian
ISBN 978-0974769233
eBook ISBN 978-0983574484

Power of Praise ©
Poetry of Spiritual Christianity ™
ISBN 978-0974769271
eBook ISBN 978-0983574477

GOD... i believe ©
Simple Steps on the Path
of Spiritual Christianity ™
ISBN 978-0974769202
eBook ISBN 978-0983574460

Erotica Series

Seduction ©
Pleasing Women Sexually
ISBN 978-0982658598
eBook ISBN 978-0983574583

Orgy of Words ©
Salacious Short Stories in Poetic Prose
ISBN 978-0982658529
eBook ISBN 978-0983574569

Self Help Series

Pathways to Publishing ©
Self Publishing
Manuscript to Publication
ISBN 978-0982658567
eBook ISBN 978-0983574507

Seduction ©
Pleasing Women Sexually
ISBN 978-0982658598
eBook ISBN 978-0983574583

GOD. . . i believe ©
Simple Steps on the Path
of Spiritual Christianity ™
ISBN 978-0974769202
eBook ISBN 978-0983574460

www.ingramcontent.com/pod-product-compliance
Lightning Source LLC
LaVergne TN
LVHW011359080426
835511LV00005B/339